I-SPY

AIRCRAFT

D1151237

This book belongs to:

I began this book on: (DATE)

I made my first I-Spy on: (DATE)

7 April 2002

I sent off for my badge on: (DATE)

To get you started on the 1000 points you need for a badge, here are a few easy spots you can make now.

In the 'Military Aircraft section, which airforce is flying the McDonnell Douglas F-4 Phantom II in our picture?
5 points for a right answer

Which of the 'Light Aircraft and Sportsplanes' has its propeller at the back and a foreplane?
5 points for a right answer

Which 'Historical Aircraft' would you never see landing on a runway?
5 points for a right answer

Which of the 'Helicopters' is just about to, or has just completed, mid-air refuelling?
5 points for a right answer

Answers on page 48

Aerospatiale/BAC Concorde

Concorde can carry 144 people at twice the speed of sound, so it is the world's only supersonic airliner. It first flew in 1969 and, at the moment, there are twelve aircraft serving with Air France and British Airways.
I-Spy for 20

Airbus Industrie A300

The A300 was the first of a family of airliners designed and built by a European consortium of companies from Britain, France, West Germany, and Spain. Powered by two turbofans, the A300 can carry up to 344 passengers and has a range of 3232 miles (5200 km).
I-Spy for 10

Airbus Industrie A310

Developed from the A300, and using the same fuselage section, the A310 has eight-abreast seating but has been shortened so that it can carry only 280 passengers.
I-Spy for 10

Airbus Industrie A320

This is the latest and the smallest of the Airbus family. It is a 180-seat, short- to medium-range airliner. It first flew in 1987 when it was the first civil airliner to feature the electronic digital 'fly-by-wire' flight-control system.
I-Spy for 10

Antonov AN-225 Mriya

The world's largest aircraft, the Mriya has a wingspan of 84.4 metres (277 ft) and is 84 metres (276 ft) long. Powered by six turbofan engines, its maximum take-off weight is 600 000 kilograms (1 322 751 lb). The Mriya (Dream) can carry piggy-back loads which are too big to fit into its cav-fuselage.
I-Spy for 50

BAC One-Eleven

A successful British airliner, the twin-engined BAC One-Eleven first flew in 1963. Early versions can accommodate 89 passengers with the later, stretched, models carrying up to 119. The One-Eleven has also been built under licence in Romania.

I-Spy for **10**

Boeing 707

The first in Boeing's series of jet airliners, it made its maiden flight in 1954. The 707 is powered by four wing-mounted turbofans. Early production versions were able to carry 181 passengers, later models up to 195.

I-Spy for **15**

Boeing 727

First flying in 1963, the 727 short/medium-range airliner makes use of the same fuselage section as the 707. It is powered by three rear-mounted turbofans and has a T-tail, tailplane placed on top of the fin and rudder.

I-Spy for **15**

Boeing 737

The most successful
jet airliner to date, this
short/medium-range
airliner is powered by
two wing-mounted
turbofans. Since its
first flight in 1967, the
737 has been
produced in several
models, with passen-
ger capacity rising
from about 100 in the
first production aircraft
to 156 in the
737-400 version.
I-Spy for 5

Boeing 747

The 'Jumbo Jet' is still the world's largest airliner even though it was first
flown in 1969. Powered by four turbofans, it was the first airliner to
feature a 'wide-body' fuselage which has up to 490 seats set
ten abreast in a high-density arrangement.
I-Spy for 5

Boeing 747 SP

The extra long-range version of the 747 features a shortened fuselage which reduces seating capacity to 360 people to save weight, thereby increasing its range to almost 9600 miles (15 400 km). What does 'SP' stand for?

I-Spy for **15**
Double with answer

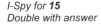

Boeing 747-400

Latest and largest in the 747 family, the -400 can be distinguished from the outside by its 'winglets'; these devices are vertical airfoils mounted at the wing-tips, and they help to reduce drag.
I-Spy for **10**

Boeing 757

The 757 was designed as a replacement for the 727, and also makes use of the same fuselage section as the 707. It is powered by two high-bypass ratio, wing-mounted turbofans. The 757 first flew in 1982, and this short/medium-haul airliner can accommodate up to 239 passengers.
I-Spy for **10**

Boeing 767
Designed at the same time as the 757 as a medium-range, high-capacity airliner, the two aircraft have much in common, but the 767 features a 'wide-body' fuselage with up to 290 passengers in eight-abreast seating.
I-Spy for 10

British Aerospace 146
This short-range, 90- to 130-seat airliner differs from its main rivals in that it is powered by four turbofans mounted beneath high-set anhedralled wings. It is noted for being one of the quietest jet airliners in service.
I-Spy for 15

British Aerospace Jetstream
British Aerospace inherited the Jetstream design when its manufacturer, Scottish Aviation, became a division of BAe in 1978. Capable of carrying nineteen passengers 736 miles (1185 km), the Jetstream 31 model is powered by two turboprops.
I-Spy for 15

Douglas DC-8

The first jet in the Douglas Commercial series of aircraft, the DC-8 competed directly with Boeing's 707 airliner and first flew in 1958, nearly four years later than the 707. Early versions were powered by four turbojets but were replaced later by turbofans.
I-Spy for **20**

Douglas DC-9 and McDonnell Douglas MD-80

First flying in 1965, this short-range airliner is powered by two turbofans mounted on either side of the rear fuselage under a T-tail. Early variants could carry up to eighty passengers, but the fuselage has been stretched several times and some models of the MD-80 series accommodate over 150 people.
I-Spy for **5**

Douglas DC-10

The wide-body DC-10 is a long-range airliner which can seat up to 323 passengers. It is powered by three turbofans, two under the wings, and one at the root of the fin and rudder. The KC-10 is a tanker/transport version operated by the United States Air Force.
*I-Spy for **10***

Embraer EMB-110 Bandeirante

Designed and built in Brazil, the Bandeirante is a nineteen-seat, short-range commuter transport aircraft. It is powered by two turboprops and can cruise at a speed of 244 mph (393 km/h). It has a range of 1191 miles (1916 km).
*I-Spy for **15***

Fokker F28 Fellowship and Fokker 100

Built in the Netherlands and powered by two rear-mounted turbofans, the F.28 short-range airliner has been increased in size throughout its life. The original F.28, which flew in 1967, could carry sixty-five passengers. How many passengers can the most recent development, the Fokker 100, carry?
*I-Spy for **15***
Double with answer

Fokker F27 Friendship and Fokker 50

This is a short-range passenger transport that first flew in 1955. As well as being built in the Netherlands, the type was licence-built in the United States by Fairchild as the FH-227. The latest version is the F-50 which, while similar in appearance, uses many composite materials in its construction.

I-Spy for 10

de Havilland Canada DHC-7

The Dash 7 as it is known, is a fifty-seat, STOL airliner. It is powered by four turboprops mounted on a high wing and also features a T-tail. The first flight was made in 1975. What does 'STOL' stand for?

_____

I-Spy for 15
Double with answer

de Havilland Canada DHC-8

The Dash 8 regional airliner is powered by two turboprops, and has a high wing and T-tail. It started life as the Dash 8-100 with thirty-nine passenger seats but the enlarged Dash 8-300 can accommodate about fifty people.

I-Spy for 20

de Havilland D H 104 Dove

A short-range passenger transport, the Dove first flew in 1945. It had a crew of two and could carry up to eleven passengers. The Royal Air Force and Royal Navy operated the type as the Devon and Sea Devon respectively.
I-Spy for 20

Ilyushin Il-62 'Classic'

The design of the Soviet Il-62 long-range airliner was influenced largely by that of the Vickers VC-10. The two aircraft share features such as the four rear-mounted turbofans, swept wing, and T-tail. The 'Classic' entered airline service with Aeroflot in 1967.
I-Spy for 15

Lockheed L-1011 Tristar

Lockheed's wide-body airliner first flew in 1970. It is powered by three turbofans, two under the wings and one in the rear fuselage with its air intake at the base of the fin. The Tristar can seat up to 400 passengers.
I-Spy for 10

SAAB 340
This thirty-five-seat, regional transport aircraft is built in Sweden and was first flown during 1983. Powered by two turboprops it has a range of about 725 miles (1167 km) at 288 mph (463 km/h).
I-Spy for 15

Short 330
Developed from the Short Skyvan, the 330 is a regional airliner which seats up to thirty passengers. It is powered by two turboprops, has twin fins and rudders, and a square-section fuselage. The C-23 Sherpa is a military transport version flown by the United States Air Force.
I-Spy for 15

Vickers Super VC10
First flying in 1962, the VC10 was designed to meet a British Overseas Airways requirement for a long-range airliner. The RAF currently operates VC10s as transports and also as in-flight refuelling tankers. How many VC10s and Super VC10s were built?

I-Spy for 20
Double with answer

Blackburn Buccaneer
Designed as a carrier-borne, low-level strike aircraft, the Buccaneer first flew in 1955. Buccaneers were transferred to the RAF in the early 1970s when the Royal Navy phased out its large aircraft carriers.
I-Spy for 15

Boeing E-3
Also known as AWACS, the E-3 is basically a Boeing 707 airliner converted into an airborne radar platform. Its crew are able to detect and track enemy aircraft, and then direct friendly fighters to intercept them. What does 'AWACS' stand for?

I-Spy for 20
Double with answer

Boeing Model 464 B-52 Stratofortress
The B-52 is capable of carrying 27 215 kilograms (60 000 lb) of conventional bombs or twelve Air Launched Cruise Missiles. It has been in service with the United States Air Force's Strategic Air Command since 1957 and saw active service in Vietnam and more recently during Operation Desert Storm — The Liberation of Kuwait.
I-Spy for 20

13

Boeing Model 717 KC-135 Stratotanker

Air-to-air refuelling is used by most air forces to increase the range of their aircraft. This flying fuel tanker, which looks very similar to the Boeing 707 airliner, is able to refuel aircraft while still airborne, using its tail-mounted flying boom.
I-Spy for 20

British Aerospace Nimrod

The Nimrod was developed from the airframe of the de Havilland Comet airliner as an antisubmarine, maritime patrol aircraft. The main external difference is that it has a deepened fuselage which contains a weapons' bay.
I-Spy for 15

British Aerospace Sea Harrier

This naval version of the Harrier, Vertical Take-Off and Landing (VTOL) fighter, was developed for the Royal Navy's three small aircraft carriers, as a multi-role fighter for air defence and attack duties. Sea Harriers performed well in combat during the Falklands Campaign of 1982.
I-Spy for 10

14

British Aerospace/ McDonnell Douglas Harrier II

A development of the world's first operational VTOL combat aircraft, the Harrier II features greater payload/range capability than earlier Harriers. It is currently flown by the RAF as the Harrier GR Mk 5 and Mk 7, and by the United States Marine Corps as the AV-8B.
I-Spy for 10

British Aerospace Hawk

Developed for the RAF as an advanced trainer, the Hawk has two seats in tandem for a pupil and instructor. It is powered by a single turbofan and is currently flown by a number of air forces around the world. Which famous display team uses this aircraft?

_____

_____

I-Spy for 10
Double with answer

Douglas A-4 Skyhawk

Nicknamed the 'Bantam Bomber', this small, single-seat carrier-borne strike aircraft is powered by one turbojet. It can carry a very heavy bomb load for its size. Over 3000 were built, including the two-seat trainer version designated TA-4.

I-Spy for 20

Fairchild Republic A-10A Thunderbolt II

Known by its pilots as the 'Warthog' because of its ungainly appearance, the A-10 is an aircraft specifically designed to attack tanks and other armoured vehicles. Its primary weapon is a multi-barrel cannon, and it is also capable of carrying bombs and missiles on underwing pylons. It is heavily armoured.

I-Spy for 10

General Dynamics F-111

This aircraft was the world's first operational variable geometry, or 'swing-wing', aircraft. First flying in 1964, it remains in service today with the United States Air Force as a long-range strike bomber.

I-Spy for 10

General Dynamics F-16 Fighting Falcon

First flown in 1974, the F-16 has become one of the west's most important warplanes and more than 3000 have been ordered by air forces around the world. As a tactical fighter, it is designed to carry air-to-air and air-to-ground weapons.

I-Spy for 5

Grumman A-6 Intruder

Designed as a carrier-borne strike aircraft, the subsonic A-6 first flew in 1960, and is still the United States Navy's most important attack plane. Some A-6 aircraft are used as in-flight refuelling tankers, and these are designated KA-6D.

I-Spy for 15

Grumman E-2C Hawkeye

The Hawkeye is designed to perform the same basic function of Airborne Early Warning as the Boeing E-3 Sentry. Powered by two tubroprops, this radar plane is flown from the United States Navy's aircraft carriers and because of the limited hangar space on-board ship it has a special feature. What?

_____

_____

I-Spy for 15
Double with answer

Grumman F-14 Tomcat
The Tomcat is United States Navy's air-defence fighter. It features variable-geometry wings, twin fins and rudders, has a crew of two, and is powered by two afterburning turbofans. With its AIM-54 air-to-air missiles, it can engage its prey at a range of over 100 miles (160 km).
I-Spy for 15

Hawker Hunter
The Hawker Hunter first flew in 1951 and became Britain's most successful post-World War 2 fighter — about 2000 were produced. Powered by a single turbojet, the Hunter has a maximum speed of around 622 mph (1000 km/h) and is armed with four 30-mm cannons.
I-Spy for 10

Lockheed C-130 Hercules
A real success story, the military transport, C-130 Hercules first flew in 1954 and remains in production today, with more than 1700 having been built. Powered by four turboprops mounted on a high wing, for ease of loading, it has a rear door ramp. A civil transport version is designated the L-100.
I-Spy for 5

Lockheed C-5 Galaxy

The largest aircraft in the United States Air Force's inventory, the C-5 has a wingspan of 68 metres (223 ft) and a fuselage length of 75.6 metres (248 ft). This long-range transport aircraft can carry up to 120 000 kilograms (265 000 lb) or 365 troops over 1874 miles (3015 km) at a speed of 506 mph (814 km/h).
I-Spy for 15

Lockheed F-104 Starfighter

The F-104, single-seat, tactical strike and reconnaissance fighter first flew in 1954. It has a wingspan of just 6.68 metres (21 ft 11 in), and is powered by a single afterburning turbojet giving it a top speed of about 1320 mph (2124 km/h).
I-Spy for 15

Lockheed F-117A
This aircraft is designed so as to be almost invisible to radar, and is therefore less likely to be detected and shot down before reaching its target. Its unusual angular shape helps to deflect radar beams and its skin is covered with radar-absorbent material.

What nickname is given to this type of aircraft? _____
I-Spy for 25 – double with answer

Lockheed P 3C Orion
Developed from the Lockheed Electra passenger plane, the Orion is a long-range patrol and anti-submarine aircraft. It is capable of patrolling for more than twelve hours at 237 mph (381 km/h), and can carry weapons such as torpedoes, depth charges, and missiles.
I-Spy for 15

MILITARY AIRCRAFT

Lockheed U-2 and TR-1

A long-range, high-altitude, reconnaissance aircraft or 'spyplane', the U-2 first flew in 1955. It is powered by a single turbojet which enables it to fly at altitudes of up to 23 927 metres (78 500 ft) for more than fifteen hours. The latest version is designated TR-1.
I-Spy for 20

McDonnell Douglas F-15 Eagle

The main air-superiority fighter of the United States Air Force, the F-15 was designed as a successor to the F-4 and first flew in 1972. A two-seat attack version, known as the F-15E Strike Eagle, has since been developed. Both are powered by two afterburning turbofans and feature twin fins and rudders.
I-Spy for 5

McDonnell Douglas F-4 Phantom II

The West's most successful post-World War 2 fighter, more than 5000 had been built when production of the F-4 ended in 1979. Powered by two turbofans, the Phantom can carry a wide range of weapons including air-to-air, and air-to-ground missiles, bombs, or rockets on its underwing pylons.
I-Spy for 5

McDonnell Douglas F/A-18 Hornet
The Hornet was developed from Northrop's YF-17 prototype which lost in the competition for USAF's lightweight fighter programme to the YF-16. The Hornet has entered service with both the United States Navy and Marine Corps, as well as with the air forces of Australia, Canada, and Spain.
*I-Spy for **10***

Mikoyan-Gurevich MiG-29
This is the latest in the long line of Soviet fighters to come from the Mikoyan design bureau. Since the end of the 'Cold War', the Soviet air-force has been happy to show off the the MiG-29 at western air shows. Its NATO code name is 'Fulcrum'.
*I-Spy for **20***

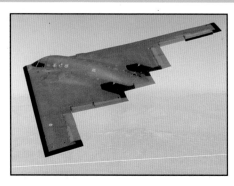

Northrop B-2
The B-2 is a long-range 'Stealth' bomber. It is a very strange shape in the sky because it is a 'flying wing' design with no proper fuselage or tail surfaces. It can carry cruise missiles and nuclear or conventional bombs.
I-Spy for 25

Panavia Tornado IDS
Planned in the 1960s as the MRCA or Multi-Role Combat Aircraft, the variable-geometry Tornado is built by an international consortium of companies from Italy, Germany and the United Kingdom. The IDS, Interdictor Strike aircraft is operated by the RAF as the Tornado GR Mk 1.
I-Spy for 5

Panavia Tornado F Mk 3 (ADV)

Developed specifically for the RAF, the Air Defence Variant of the Tornado is larger than the IDS aircraft because it carries more internal fuel. It can be armed with four Skyflash and four Sidewinder air-to-air missiles and has an internal 27-mm cannon.

I-Spy for **5**

SEPECAT Jaguar

An Anglo-French consortium, SEPECAT, was formed for the design and construction of the Jaguar low-level strike fighter. Royal Air Force and French Armée de l'Air Jaguars saw active service during the 1991 Gulf War.

I-Spy for **5**

Short Tucano

Developed from the Embraer EMB-312 Tucano, this aircraft is to replace the Jet Provost as the Royal Air Force's basic trainer. It features a more powerful turboprop engine than the earlier Brazilian aircraft.

I-Spy for **10**

Sukhoi Su-27

The Su-27 air-superiority fighter, NATO code-named 'Flanker', looks very similar to the MiG-29 but is, in fact, a much larger aircraft. Like most modern western fighters, the Soviet-built 'Flanker' features an electronic 'fly-by-wire' system.

I-Spy for **20**

British Aerospace 125

An executive transport or 'Bizjet', the 125 has undergone continuous improvements since its first flight in 1962, and can now transport up to fourteen passengers over 3000 miles (5000 km).

I-Spy for 10

Canadair 601 Challenger

One of the largest 'Bizjets' around, the Challenger has a crew of two and can seat up to nineteen passengers; it has a maximum cruise speed of 506 mph (815 km/h). The prototype was first flown in 1986.

I-Spy for 15

27

Cessna Citation I, II, and III

When first introduced, this seven/eight-seat, turbofan-powered, executive transport was called the Fanjet 500, later the Citation 500, and finally the Citation I. An enlarged development, the Citation II, followed. Cessna also build the Citation III 'bizjet' which is an entirely new aircraft with swept wings.

I-Spy for **15**

Learjet 35

Derived from the earlier series 20 Learjets, the 35, like all Learjets to date, is powered by two rear-mounted turbofans and features wingtip-mounted fuel tanks. More than 650 have now been built.

I-Spy for **15**

Embraer Ipanema
Not known for their beauty, agricultural aircraft are used primarily for spraying crops with pesticides. They are simple to operate and maintain, and they need to be very rugged.
I-Spy for 20

Cessna Models 150 and 152
This two-seat, high-wing, light aircraft was first flown in 1957. In 1966, the 150F introduced a swept fin and rudder. The 152 has a more powerful piston engine but is otherwise similar to the earlier 150. It is now commonly used by flying clubs around the world to train pilots.
I-Spy for 5

Cessna Models 170, 172, 175, and 182
The most successful lightplane series to date, the four-set, piston-engined Cessna 170 first flew in 1948. Early aircraft in this family featured a tailwheel-type undercarraige but, from the model 170B of 1955, tricycle landing gear was fitted.
I-Spy for 5

Cessna Models 310

A five/six-seat, low-wing, twin piston-engined monoplane, the Cessna 310 first flew in 1952. It was developed continuously throughout its production life. What is the most noticeable feature of this aircraft?

*I-Spy for **10***
Double with answer ☑

Cessna 336/337 Skymaster

This unusual four/six-seat aircraft is powered by two piston engines, one mounted at either end of a fuselage nacelle. The tailplane is mounted on twin booms from the high wing. The model 336 has a fixed tricycle undercarriage whereas that of the 337 is retractable. ☑
*I-Spy for **20***

Columban Cricri

First flown in 1973, the Cricri is one of the smallest twin-engined aircraft in the world. It has a wingspan of 4.9 metres (16 ft), a length of 3.91 metres (12 ft 10 in), and an empty weight of just 80 kilograms (176 lb). Despite its size, the Cricri can perform aerobatics.
*I-Spy for **20***

de Havilland Canada DHC-1 Chipmunk
A two-place, tandem-seat basic trainer, the DHC-1 was designed and
produced by de Havilland Canada. The majority of Chipmunks were built
by de Havilland in England, however, when the type was ordered
in quantity by the RAF to replace the Tiger Moth.
I-Spy for 15

Piper J-3 Cub and Super Cub
This is a tandem, two-seat, high-wing light aircraft which first flew in
1930 as the Taylor Cub. It was the first aircraft to be produced by Piper
when they bought out the Taylor Brothers in 1937. The Super
Cub was certificated in 1949.
I-Spy for 10

LIGHT AIRCRAFT AND SPORTSPLANES

Piper PA-28 Cherokee

The Cherokee family started with the PA-28 in 1960 and has been produced in many forms — the Cherokee 140 two-seater and the 180 four-seater are the basic models. The PA-32 Cherokee six, a six-seater was introduced in 1963. Other versions include the Cherokee Arrows with retractable undercarriage.
I-Spy for 5

Piper PA-23 Aztec

The Aztec was developed from the PA-23 Apache four/five-seat light twin, and is itself a six seater. It was first built in 1959 and remained in production until 1982.
I-Spy for 10

Piper PA-31 Navajo
A twin piston-engined, six/ten-seat, executive or commuter aircraft, the PA-31 Navajo entered production in 1967. Later models include the Navajo Chieftain with stretched fuselage and turbo-supercharged engines.
I-Spy for 10

Pitts Special
The biplane Pitts Special is a highly successful aerobatic sportsplane. The single-seat S-1 was first flown in 1947 and later it was also built as the two-seater S-2. Both versions have a wingspan of just 5.28 metres (17 ft 4 in).
I-Spy for 10

Rutan Vari EZ and Long EZ
This unorthodox two-seat, home-built, light aircraft is constructed largely of fibreglass. It is a canard design, with a foreplane in front of the main wing. It has a rear-mounted engine driving a pusher propeller, and also features fixed main wheels but a retractable nose-wheel.
I-Spy for 15

LIGHT AIRCRAFT AND SPORTSPLANES

Weight-shift Microlights

Designed as recreational flying machines which are relatively cheap to operate, these aircraft are basically powered hang-gliders. They have a 'trike' unit which forms the pilot's seat and holds the engine, suspended below what is known as a 'flexwing'.
I-Spy for 5

Gliders and Sailplanes

Gliders do not have engines to power them. They are usually towed into the air by a powered plane and, once cast off from that aircraft, it is the skill of the pilot which enables the glider to stay aloft for long periods, using rising currents of air to gain altitude.
I-Spy for 5

Avro Lancaster
Britain's finest heavy bomber of World War 2, the Lancaster was a four-engined development of the unsuccessful twin-engined Avro Manchester. Heavily modified Lancasters were used in the famous 'Dam Busters' raid on Germany using the Barnes-Wallace-designed 'bouncing bomb'.

I-Spy for **15**

Avro Vulcan
Developed as one of the RAF's nuclear 'V-bombers', the Vulcan first flew in 1952. About thirty years later, it was to see active service during the Falklands War dropping conventional bombs on the airfield at Port Stanley.
I-Spy for **15**

Beechcraft Model 18
First flown in 1937, this twin-engined, light passenger executive, transport aircraft stayed in production for thirty-two years. It has twin fins and rudders and a tail-wheel type undercarriage. Even today, many are still flying in various parts of the world.
I-Spy for **15**

HISTORICAL AIRCRAFT

Boeing B-17 Fortress

One of the United States' most important aircraft of World War 2, the B-17 four-engined, long-range bomber was first flown in 1935. The most numerous variant built was the B-17G which was armed with no less than twelve 0.5-inch (1.27-cm) machine-guns for defence.
I-Spy for 10

Consolidated Model 28 PBY Catalina

Designed as a long-range patrol flying boat, the PBY first flew in 1935. It is a strut-braced, parasol-wing monoplane with a span of 31.7 metres (104 ft) and is powered by two radial engines. Later models were amphibious because they were fitted with a retractable tricycle undercarriage.
I-Spy for 10

Douglas DC-3, C-47 and Dakota

This was one of the most important airliners ever built. First flying in 1935 as the Douglas Sleeper Transport, the DC-3 saw large-scale service during World War 2 in the United States military as the C-47 and in the RAF as the Dakota. After the War, many DC-3s returned to civilian use, and still operate today.
I-Spy for 5

Fairey Swordfish
The Swordfish carrier-borne torpedo bomber was used by the Royal Navy all through World War 2 despite being an obsolete design. It had a maximum speed of just 154 mph (248 km/h). What nickname was affectionately given to this aircraft?
I-Spy for 15 – double with answer

Gloster Meteor
The Meteor was the only Allied jet fighter to see active service during World War 2. The first prototype flew in 1943, with production aircraft joining RAF squadrons in the following year. Later Marks remained in service until the late 1950s.
I-Spy for 10

de Havilland DH 82 Tiger Moth

Developed from the DH 60T Moth Trainer, the first DH 82 Tiger Moth was flown in 1931. The RAF soon ordered it as a basic trainer and, by the time production finished, more than 7000 had been built. Many of these beautiful old biplanes are still flying today.
I-Spy for 5

de Havilland Mosquito

The Mosquito was designed as a high-speed light bomber and, because of its wooden construction, and amazing speed and versatility, it became known as the 'Wooden Wonder'. The Mosquito also served as a night-fighter, photo-reconnaissance aircraft and trainer.
I-Spy for 20

Hawker Hurricane
This was the most numerous fighter in the RAF at the time of the Battle of Britain. Well known for its rugged construction, the Hurricane remained in service throughout the war, and was used later in a ground-attack role.
I-Spy for 15

Hawker Sea Fury
Last of Hawker's family of piston-engined fighters, the Sea Fury arrived too late to fight in World War 2. It did see active service with the Royal Navy and the navies of Canada and Australia, however, during the Korean War of 1950-53.
I-Spy for 15

Junkers Ju 52/3m
The main German transport aircraft of World War 2, it was powered by three radial engines and has a fixed, tailwheel-type undercarriage. The fuselage and wings are constructed largely of corrugated alloy panels.
I-Spy for 20

North American P-51 Mustang

This was one of the great fighters of World War 2. Not only was it fast and manoeuvrable, but it also had a long enough range to enable it to escort American bombers on their hazardous daylight raids on Germany. Models from the P-51D onwards featured a cut-down rear fuselage and 'tear drop' cockpit canopy.

I-Spy for 10

North American T-6 Texan

With around 17 000 aircraft built, the T-6, or Harvard as it was called in RAF service, was the most important Allied advanced trainer of World War 2. One of its most distinctive features is the noise made by its propeller tips when travelling supersonic.

I-Spy for 5

Republic P-47 Thunderbolt

A large and heavyweight World War 2 fighter, the XP-47B first flew in 1941. This led to the production versions P-47B and P-47C of which about 770 were built. More than 12 600 of the main variant, the P-47D, were made.

I-Spy for 15

Short Sunderland
First flying in 1937, the
Sunderland became the
RAF's main maritime
patrol flying boat of
World War 2. It had a
range of 2690 miles
(4320 km) and could
carry 908 kilograms
(2000 lb) of bombs or
depth charges which it
would use to attack
enemy submarines.
I-Spy for **20**

Supermarine Spitfire
Probably the best-known fighter of all time, the Spitfire first flew in 1936.
It remained in production throughout World War 2 and was developed
continuously with ever-more powerful engines. Well over 20 000
had been built by the end of the war.
I-Spy for **10**

HELICOPTERS

Aerospatiale AS 350 and AS 355 Ecureuil

This is a five- to six-seat, French-built, general-purpose helicopter. The AS 350 version is powered by a single turboshaft engine whereas the AS 355 Ecureuil 2 has two engines.
I-Spy for 10

Aerospatiale SA 365 Dauphin 2

This is a multipurpose helicopter capable of civil and military roles. Instead of a conventional tail rotor, it has a distinctive 'Fenestron' antitorque tail rotor in the tail fin.
I-Spy for 15

Agusta 109

This eight-seat, Italian-designed and built, light utility helicopter is powered by two turboshaft engines which give it a cruise speed of about 173 mph (278 km/h) and a range of 392 miles (631 km).
I-Spy for 15

Bell Model 47
This piston-engined helicopter first flew in 1945, and later became the first helicopter to receive civil certification. Many different models were built for civil and for military uses, and, from the 47D model on, all featured the distinctive 'goldfish bowl' cockpit.
I-Spy for 15

Bell Model 206 Jet Ranger
Originally designed as scout helicopter for the United States Army, the five-seat Jet Ranger has since become one of the world's most successful civil helicopters. A stretched and more powerful version, known as the 206L Long Ranger, is able to carry seven people.
I-Spy for 5

Bell Model 222
Powered by two turboshaft engines, this eight-seat light commercial helicopter has a cruise speed of about 165 mph (265 km/h). Distinguishing features include low-mounted sponsons either side of the fuselage and a wide-cord, two-blade main rotor.
I-Spy for 10

Boeing Vertol Chinook
This large, twin-rotor helicopter first flew in 1961 and remains in service today in both civil and military forms. Its intermeshing rotors, mounted in tandem, each have a diameter of 18.29 metres (60 ft).
I-Spy for 15

McDonnell Douglas 500

This light utility helicopter was developed by Hughes for the United States Army as the OH-6. Hughes was later taken over by McDonnell Douglas which now builds the helicopter. Over 4000 of the civil and military versions have been built since its first flight in 1963.

I-Spy for 10

McDonnell Douglas AH-64 Apache

This formidable anti-tank attack helicopter is now in service with the United States Army and proved very successful during Operation Desert Storm in 1991. It is armed with a 30-mm cannon and can carry up to sixteen Hellfire laser-guided anti-armour missiles.

I-Spy for 20

HELICOPTERS

Sikorsky S-61 Sea King — H-3

The S-61 was designed as an anti-submarine helicopter and first flew in 1959. It has since been produced in the United States by Sikorsky, in Italy by Agusta, Japan by Mitsubishi, and in the United Kingdom by Westland. Military and civil transport S-61 versions have also been built.

I-Spy for 10

Sikorsky S-65 — H-53

The West's largest helicopter to date, with a rotor diameter of 24.08 metres (79 ft), the CH-53 Sea Stallion is capable of carrying fifty-five troops. Initial versions were powered by two turboshaft engines but some later variants have three.

I-Spy for 20

Sikorsky S-76 Spirit
A light commercial
transport helicopter,
the S-76 is powered
by two turboshaft
engines and can carry
up to twelve passen-
gers. It has a very
streamlined shape
and has retractable
undercarriage. A
military version, the
H-76 Eagle, has
also been sold.
I-Spy for 20

Westland Lynx
The Lynx is built in
two main production
versions: a ship-borne
anti-submarine
helicopter which has a
tricycle, wheeled
undercarriage, and a
land-based military
utility and anti-armour
version which
has skids.
I-Spy for 10

47

INDEX

© I-Spy Limited 1999

ISBN: 1 85671 215 X
Michelin Tyre Public Limited Company
Edward Hyde Building, 38 Clarendon Road, Watford, Herts WD1 1SX

MICHELIN and the Michelin Man are Registered Trademarks of Michelin

A CIP record for this title is available from the British Library.

Edited by Neil Curtis. Designed by Richard Garratt.

The Publisher gratefully acknowledges the contribution of Brian Trodd Publishing House Limited who provided the majority of the photographs in this I-Spy book. Text by Nikk Burridge.

Colour reproduction by Anglia Colour Ltd.

Printed in Spain by Graficromo SA.

48

Answers
Title page: Luftwaffe of Germany; Rutan Vari EZ and Long EZ; Short Sunderland; Sikorsky S-65 —H-53; Boeing 747 SP; Special Performance. Fokker F28 Fellowship and Fokker 100: 107. de Havilland Canada DHC-7: Short Take-Off and Landing. Vickers Super VC10: 54. Boeing E-3: Airborne Early Warning and Control System; British Aerospace Hawk: The Red Arrows. Grumman E-2C Hawkeye: Folding wings. Lockheed F-117A: 'Stealth'. Cessna Models 310: Wing-mounted fuel tanks. Fairey Swordfish: 'String Bag'.